Log Cabin

The Classic Quilt Series #3

LAURA NOWNES

The Quilt Digest Press ✳ *San Francisco*

Editorial and production direction by Michael Kile.
Book editing by Harold Nadel.
Book and cover design by Kajun Graphics.
Quilt photography by Sharon Risedorph and Karen
Steffens.
Cover and room setting photographs by Sharon
Risedorph.
Computer graphics by Kandy Petersen.
Typographical composition by DC Typography.
Printed by Nissha Printing Company, Ltd., Kyoto, Japan.
Color separations by the printer.

*For Diana, with love and thanks for her encouragement
and support.*

First Printing.

Library of Congress Cataloging-in-Publication Data

Nownes, Laura, 1953-
　　Log cabin / Laura Nownes.
　　　　p.　　cm.
　　ISBN 0-913327-24-7 (paper) : $6.95
　　1. Quilting–Patterns. 2. Patchwork–Patterns. I. Title.
TT835.N69　1990
746.9'7– dc20
　　　　　　　　　　　　　　　　　　　　　90-41882
　　　　　　　　　　　　　　　　　　　　　　　　CIP

The Quilt Digest Press
955 Fourteenth Street
San Francisco 94114

INTRODUCTION

Few quilt patterns, if any, create as immediate a connection to tradition as *Log Cabin* in its many variations. A *Log Cabin* quilt links us to our quiltmaking past as well as our pioneering history.

Here are five *Log Cabin* quilts, each representing one of the five major pattern variations: *Barn Raising, Straight Furrow, Courthouse Steps, Light and Dark* and *Zig Zag.* If you are unfamiliar with the infinite variety of patterns and styles available to the *Log Cabin* maker by the mere manipulation of colors, light and dark, on the quilt's surface, take a few minutes to study the five quilts presented here.

Then, hard as it is, choose one for your quilt project. Once you've done so, you'll find each quilt has:
- A full-color photograph
- A bed and wall-size chart
- A yardage chart
- Cutting and sewing instructions
- Accurate templates

Enjoy yourself as you add to the rich tradition of *Log Cabin* quiltmaking.

Happy quilting!

Laura

Laura Nownes

LET'S MAKE IT

Ease of construction makes the *Log Cabin* one of the most popular quilts and, with its many variations, appealing to both the beginner and the experienced quiltmaker. By using quick-cutting and time-saving sewing techniques, you can complete these quilts successfully and quickly. After you have mastered the basic construction techniques, you can arrange your blocks to make one of the five *Log Cabin* variations presented in this book.

Use the helpful chart which gives mattress sizes and suggested quilt sizes. With the exception of the crib quilt, all suggested quilt sizes allow for a 14″ drop on three sides. It is always advisable to measure your bed or wall space to determine the desired size you would like to make. Then look at the chart accompanying the pattern you have chosen and select the quilt size which comes closest to your desired finished size.

Read through the instructions and review the diagrams for the quilt you wish to make. Cut your fabric, organize your work area and you are ready to start.

Mattress size	Suggested quilt size
Crib: 27″ × 52″	45″ × 60″
Twin: 39″ × 75″	67″ × 89″
Double: 54″ × 75″	82″ × 89″
Queen: 60″ × 80″	88″ × 94″
King: 76″ × 80″	104″ × 94″
California King: 72″ × 84″	100″ × 98″

WHAT YOU NEED

Fabric: 100% cotton—see individual quilts
   for exact amounts
Sewing machine or hand sewing needle
100% cotton thread—in a color to blend with
   your fabrics
8″ fabric scissors or rotary cutter, wide plastic
   ruler and cutting board
Small scissors for clipping threads
Steam iron
Pressing surface
Batting

GETTING ORGANIZED

Any problems occurring in the construction of this block generally result from the strips (logs) being sewn in the wrong order. To avoid this problem, take time to organize your fabrics and work place before you begin. On page 7 you will find diagrams of the order in which your strips should be arranged for ease of sewing. Consult the construction diagrams often, making sure your units are positioned correctly before attaching each new strip.

Many people (myself included) do not have the luxury of a separate work area where fabric strips can be set up and remain undisturbed for an extended period of time. The solution that works for me is to lay all of my strips in the proper order on my cutting board (or large piece of cardboard). When it is time to clear the area, I can simply pick up and move the entire board, and the strips remain undisturbed.

I also have a small pressing board (approximately 18″ × 18″) covered with a light-colored towel accessible at the same table as my sewing machine; frequent pressing helps to produce neat, flat blocks quickly. (The towel on the pressing surface prevents the seams from creating a ridge on the front side of your blocks.)

CUTTING YOUR FABRIC

Using either traditional cutting with a pair of scissors or quick-cutting techniques with a rotary cutter, wide plastic ruler and cutting board, cut all of your fabrics (except borders) into the required strip sizes. Refer to the individual patterns and templates for sizes.

MAKING YOUR BLOCKS

All *Log Cabin* blocks are constructed using one of the two methods described below, working from the center of the block out to the edge. The arrangement of the blocks creates the different variations.

The basic *Log Cabin* block is divided in half diagonally, with light fabrics on one side and dark on the other. The *Courthouse Steps* variation is divided into quarters diagonally with light and dark fabrics in opposite quarters.

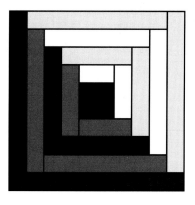

Basic Log Cabin

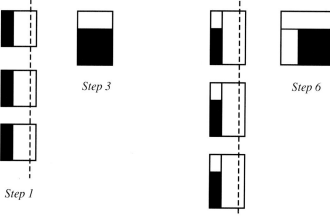

Step 1

Step 3

Step 4

Step 6

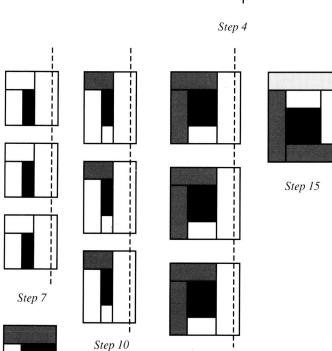

Step 7

Step 9

Step 10

Step 12

Step 13

Step 15

Basic Log Cabin Block

Use a ¼″ seam for all block construction.

1. With their right sides together, sew a strip of the first light log to each center square. To save time and thread, feed one unit directly behind the next through your sewing machine. Do not break the chain connecting the units. It is *very* important that the top and bottom edges of the fabric pieces line up perfectly. To prevent pieces from slipping, you can secure them with a pin.

2. Clip the threads between the units.

3. Press the seams away from the center squares. Then position the units in a stack, right sides facing up.

4. With their right sides together, sew a strip of the second light log to each unit. Feed one unit directly behind the next, as shown.

5. Clip the threads between the units.

6. Press the seams away from the center squares. Then position the units in a stack, right sides facing up, as shown.

7. With their right sides together, sew a strip of the first dark log to each unit. Feed one unit directly behind the next, as shown.

8. Clip the threads between the units.

9. Press the seams away from the center squares. Then position the units in a stack, right sides facing up, as shown.

10. With their right sides together, sew a strip of the second dark log to each unit. Feed one unit directly behind the next, as shown.

11. Clip the threads between the units.

12. Press the seams away from the center squares. Then position the units in a stack, right sides facing up, as shown.

13. With their right sides together, sew a strip of the third light log to each unit. Feed one unit directly behind the next, as shown.

14. Clip the threads between the units.

15. Press the seams away from the center squares. Then position the units in a stack, right sides facing up, as shown.

16. Using the same technique, sew a strip of the fourth light log to each unit. Then, clip the threads between units and press.

17. Attach the next two dark strips and then the next two light strips, in the same manner.

18. Continue attaching strips, alternating two dark, two light, and then two dark, to complete each block.

19. All of your blocks are now complete, neatly pressed and ready to be joined into a quilt top. Refer to the quilt you have selected for the block assembly diagrams.

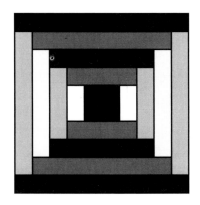

Courthouse Steps

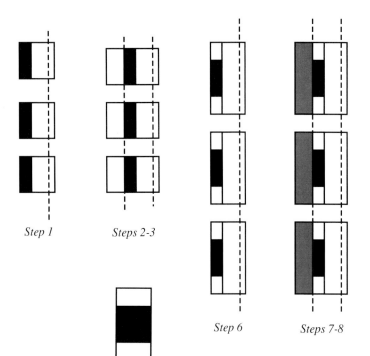

Step 1 *Steps 2-3* *Step 6* *Steps 7-8*

Step 5

Courthouse Steps Block

Use a ¼" seam for all block construction.

1. With their right sides together, sew a strip of the first light log to each center square. To save time and thread, feed one unit directly behind the next through your sewing machine. Do not break the chain connecting the units. It is *very* important that the top and bottom edges of the fabric pieces line up perfectly. To prevent pieces from slipping, you can secure them with a pin.

2. Press the seams away from the center squares.

3. Starting with the last unit sewn in Step 1, attach a light log strip of the same fabric to the opposite side of each unit, as shown. Note that the chain is still joining the units.

4. Clip the threads between the units.

5. Press the seams away from the center squares. Then position your units in a stack, right sides facing up, as shown.

6. With their right sides together, sew a strip of the first dark log to each unit, as shown.

7. Press the seams away from the center squares. Do not cut the chain connecting the units.

8. Starting with the last unit sewn in Step 6, attach a dark log strip of the same fabric to the opposite side of each unit, as shown.

9. Clip the threads between the units.

10. Press the seams away from the center squares. Then position your units in a stack, right sides facing up, as shown.

11. With their right sides together, sew a strip of the next light log to each unit, as shown.

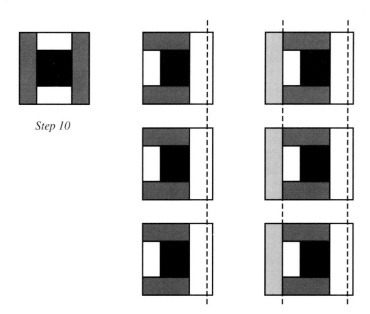

Step 10

Step 11

Steps 12-13

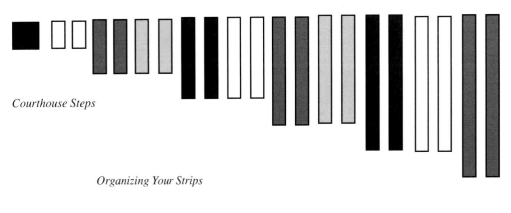

Step 15

12. Press the seams away from the center squares. Do not cut the chain connecting the units.

13. Using the technique described in Step 3, sew a light log strip of the same fabric used in Step 11 to the opposite sides of each unit, as shown.

14. Clip the threads between the units.

15. Press the seams away from the center squares. Then position your units in a stack, right sides facing up, as shown.

16. Using the same technique, attach the next two dark strips and then the next two light strips.

17. Continue attaching strips, alternating dark and then light, until all required log strips have been attached.

18. All of your blocks are now complete, neatly pressed and ready to be joined into a quilt top. Refer to the quilt you have selected for the block assembly diagrams.

Courthouse Steps

Organizing Your Strips

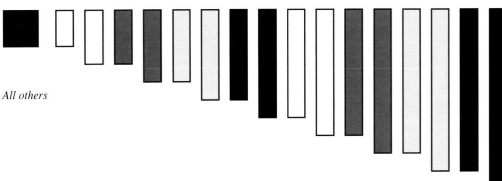

All others

BARN RAISING

Maker unknown, c.1900. Collection of Robert and Ardis James.

Although many different fabrics are used, in each block each fabric is used twice. For example, the first and second light fabrics are the same, and the first and second dark fabrics are the same.

9¼″ Block	CRIB	TWIN	DOUBLE	QUEEN	KING
Finished size	47″ × 65½″	65½″ × 84″	84″ × 84″	84″ × 102½″	102½″ × 102½″
Blocks set	4 × 6	6 × 8	8 × 8	8 × 10	10 × 10
Total blocks	24	48	64	80	100

FABRIC NEEDED (YARDS)

Note: Additional fabric is given to allow for pieced borders.

Center square	¼	⅜	⅜	½	½
Light logs	3	4	4⅝	5½	6⅝
Dark logs	3¼	4⅝	5	6	7¼
Backing	4	5	7½	9	9
Binding	⅜	½	⅝	¾	1

CUTTING YOUR FABRIC

Use Templates B1–B14

Center: Template B1, number of 2¼″ squares	24	48	64	80	100
Template B2, light, number of 1¼″ × 2¼″ pieces	24	48	64	80	100
Template B3, light and dark, number of 1¼″ × 3″ pieces, *each*	24	48	64	80	100
Template B4, light and dark, number of 1¼″ × 3¾″ pieces, *each*	24	48	64	80	100
Template B5, light and dark, number of 1¼″ × 4½″ pieces, *each*	24	48	64	80	100
Template B6, light and dark, number of 1¼″ × 5¼″ pieces, *each*	24	48	64	80	100
Template B7, light and dark, number of 1¼″ × 6″ pieces, *each*	24	48	64	80	100
Template B8, light and dark, number of 1¼″ × 6¾″ pieces, *each*	24	48	64	80	100
Template B9, light and dark, number of 1¼″ × 7½″ pieces, *each*	24	48	64	80	100
Template B10, light and dark, number of 1¼″ × 8¼″ pieces, *each*	24	48	64	80	100
Template B11, light and dark, number of 1¼″ × 9″ pieces, *each*	24	48	64	80	100
Template B12, dark, number of 1¼″ × 9¾″ pieces	24	48	64	80	100
Backing: Number of lengths	2	2	2	3	3

Pieced border: Use the remaining fabric to cut pieces with **Template B13** (1¼″ × 5½″) and **Template B14** (1½″ × 5½″).

PUTTING IT ALL TOGETHER

1. Arrange your fabric pieces as shown on page 7.

2. Construct the required number of blocks, using the technique described for the Basic *Log Cabin* Block.

3. Sew the blocks together in rows, referring to the *Barn Raising* setting shown. Double check the placement of the light and dark strips with the illustration before sewing.

4. For the pieced borders, join enough fabric pieces together to match the measurement of each side of the quilt top *plus 14″*. (This excess length is necessary to miter the corners.)

5. Stitch the pieced borders to the quilt top.

6. Miter the corners and trim the excess border length.

7. Your quilt top is ready to be hand quilted, machine quilted or tied.

8. Finish the edges with a ¼″ binding.

LIGHT AND DARK / ZIG ZAG

Maker unknown, c.1880-1900. Collection of Robert and Ardis James.

10½" Block	CRIB/ WALL	TWIN	DOUBLE/ QUEEN	KING
Finished size	49″ × 49″	70″ × 91″	91″ × 91″	112″ × 91″
Blocks set	4 × 4	6 × 8	8 × 8	10 × 8
Total blocks	16	48	64	80
FABRIC NEEDED (YARDS)				
Center square	⅛	⅛	¼	¼
Light logs	1¾	3⅞	5⅛	6¼

Dark logs	2	$4\frac{1}{4}$	$5\frac{1}{2}$	$6\frac{3}{4}$
Backing	3	$5\frac{1}{2}$	8	8
Binding	$\frac{3}{8}$	$\frac{1}{2}$	$\frac{5}{8}$	$\frac{3}{4}$

CUTTING YOUR FABRIC

Use Templates D1–D17

Center: Template D1, number of $2\frac{1}{4}''$ squares	16	48	64	80
Template D2, light, number of $1\frac{1}{8}'' \times 2\frac{1}{4}''$ pieces	16	48	64	80
Template D3, light and dark, number of $1\frac{1}{8}'' \times 2\frac{7}{8}''$ pieces, *each*	16	48	64	80
Template D4, light and dark, number of $1\frac{1}{8}'' \times 3\frac{1}{2}''$ pieces, *each*	16	48	64	80
Template D5, light and dark, number of $1\frac{1}{8}'' \times 4\frac{1}{8}''$ pieces, *each*	16	48	64	80
Template D6, light and dark, number of $1\frac{1}{8}'' \times 4\frac{3}{4}''$ pieces, *each*	16	48	64	80
Template D7, light and dark, number of $1\frac{1}{8}'' \times 5\frac{3}{8}''$ pieces, *each*	16	48	64	80
Template D8, light and dark, number of $1\frac{1}{8}'' \times 6''$ pieces, *each*	16	48	64	80
Template D9, light and dark, number of $1\frac{1}{8}'' \times 6\frac{5}{8}''$ pieces, *each*	16	48	64	80
Template D10, light and dark, number of $1\frac{1}{8}'' \times 7\frac{1}{4}''$ pieces, *each*	16	48	64	80
Template D11, light and dark, number of $1\frac{1}{8}'' \times 7\frac{7}{8}''$ pieces, *each*	16	48	64	80
Template D12, light and dark, number of $1\frac{1}{8}'' \times 8\frac{1}{2}''$ pieces, *each*	16	48	64	80
Template D13, light and dark, number of $1\frac{1}{8}'' \times 9\frac{1}{8}''$ pieces, *each*	16	48	64	80
Template D14, light and dark, number of $1\frac{1}{8}'' \times 9\frac{3}{4}''$ pieces, *each*	16	48	64	80
Template D15, light and dark, number of $1\frac{1}{8}'' \times 10\frac{3}{8}''$ pieces, *each*	16	48	64	80
Template D16, dark, number of $1\frac{1}{8}'' \times 11''$ pieces	16	48	64	80
Backing: number of lengths	1	2	3	3
Pieced border:	Use the remaining fabric to cut **Template D17** pieces.			

PUTTING IT ALL TOGETHER

1. Arrange your fabric pieces as shown on page 7.

2. Construct the required number of blocks using the technique described for the Basic *Log Cabin* Block.

3. Sew the blocks together in rows, referring to the light and dark setting shown. Double check the placement of the light and dark strips with the illustration before sewing.

4. For the pieced borders, join enough template D17 pieces to match the measurement of one side of the quilt top *plus 2"*. *Note: The template D17 pieces have deliberately been made too long so that you will not have to worry about keeping the angled edges exactly in line when joining pieces. Press the pieced strips and then even off the edges to measure $4\frac{1}{4}''$.*

5. Make two such strips and sew them to the joined blocks, being careful not to stretch them.

6. Trim the excess border lengths even with the adjacent sides of the quilt top.

7. Join enough Template D17 pieces to match the measurement of one of the remaining two sides of the quilt top *plus 2"*.

8. Make two such strips and sew them to the quilt top.

9. Trim the excess border lengths even with the other two sides of the quilt top.

10. Your quilt top is ready to be hand quilted, machine quilted or tied.

11. Finish the edges with a $\frac{1}{4}''$ binding.

AMISH LIGHT AND DARK

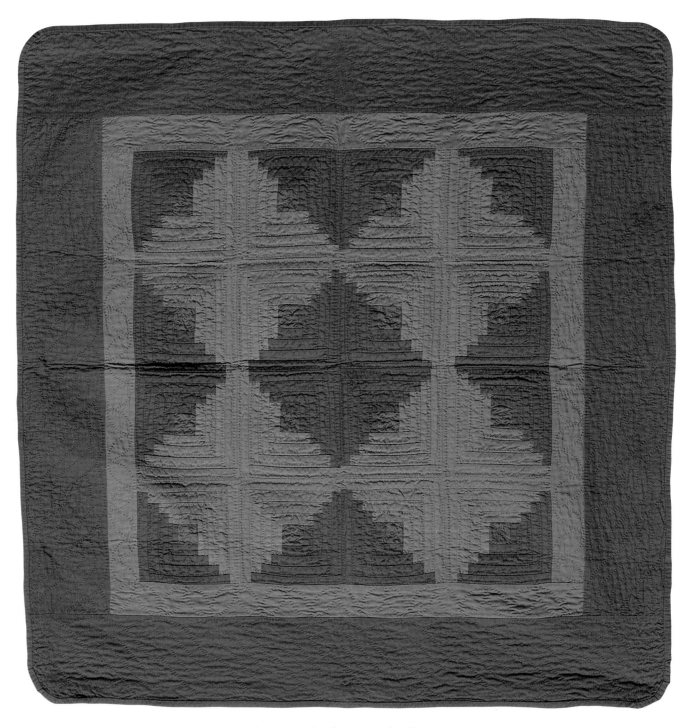

Amish maker unknown, c.1940. The Esprit Quilt Collection, San Francisco.

5⅜″ Block	WALL OR CRIB
Finished size	35″ × 35″
Blocks set	4 × 4
Total blocks	16

FABRIC NEEDED (YARDS)

Center square	⅛
Light	1
Dark *(includes binding)*	1
Backing	1¼

CUTTING YOUR FABRIC

Use Templates A1–A10

Center: Template A1, number of 1⅞″ squares	16
Template A2, dark, number of 1″ × 1⅞″ pieces	16
Template A3, light and dark, number of 1″ × 2⅜″ pieces, *each*	16
Template A4, light and dark, number of 1″ × 2⅞″ pieces, *each*	16
Template A5, light and dark, number of 1″ × 3⅜″ pieces, *each*	16
Template A6, light and dark, number of 1″ × 3⅞″ pieces, *each*	16
Template A7, light and dark, number of 1″ × 4⅜″ pieces, *each*	16
Template A8, light and dark, number of 1″ × 4⅞″ pieces, *each*	16
Template A9, light and dark, number of 1″ × 5⅜″ pieces, *each*	16
Template A10, light, number of 1″ × 5⅞″ pieces	16
Inside border:	Two at 2½″ × 22″
	Two at 2½″ × 26″
Outside border:	Two at 5¼″ × 26″
	Two at 5¼″ × 35″
Backing: number of lengths	1

PUTTING IT ALL TOGETHER

1. Arrange your fabric pieces as shown on page 7.

2. Construct 16 blocks using the technique described for the Basic *Log Cabin* Block.

3. Sew all blocks together, referring to the illustration. Double check the placement of the light and dark strips with the illustration before sewing.

4. Attach the inside and then the outside borders.

5. Your quilt top is ready to be hand quilted, machine quilted or tied.

6. Finish the edges with a ¼″ binding.

STRAIGHT FURROW

Maker unknown, c.1900. Collection of Levi Strauss & Company, San Francisco.

6″ Block	CRIB	TWIN	DOUBLE/ QUEEN	KING
Finished size	40″×58″	70″×88″	82″×88″	100″×94″
Blocks set	5×8	10×13	12×13	15×14
Total blocks	40	130	156	210

FABRIC NEEDED (YARDS)

Center square	¼	⅜	⅜	½
Light *(includes binding)*	2	3¾	4¼	5⅝
Dark	1¾	3¾	4½	5⅞
Backing	1¾	5¼	5¼	8¼

CUTTING YOUR FABRIC

Borders: Light and dark, *each*				
Four at 1¾″ ×	32″	62″	74″	92″
Four at 1¾″ ×	60″	90″	90″	96″
Use Templates F1–F8				
Center: Template F1, number of 2″ squares	40	130	156	210
Template F2, light, number of 1¼″ × 2″ pieces	40	130	156	210
Template F3, light and dark, number of 1¼″ × 2¾″ pieces, *each*	40	130	156	210
Template F4, light and dark, number of 1¼″ × 3½″ pieces, *each*	40	130	156	210
Template F5, light and dark, number of 1¼″ × 4¼″ pieces, *each*	40	130	156	210
Template F6, light and dark, number of 1¼″ × 5″ pieces, *each*	40	130	156	210
Template F7, light and dark, number of 1¼″ × 5¾″ pieces, *each*	40	130	156	210
Template F8, dark, number of 1¼″ × 6½″ pieces	40	130	156	210
Backing: number of lengths	1	2	2	3

PUTTING IT ALL TOGETHER

1. Arrange your fabric pieces as shown on page 7.

2. Construct the required number of blocks, using the technique described for the Basic *Log Cabin* Block.

3. Sew the blocks together in rows, referring to the *Straight Furrow* illustration. Double check the placement of the light and dark strips with the illustration before sewing.

4. Join four border strips together for each side of the quilt top, alternating dark and light strips.

5. Attach the top and bottom joined border strips to the blocks. The dark strips are next to the blocks, and the light strips are on the outer edge of the quilt top. *Note: Border strips have been deliberately cut too long to allow for any variation in block size. After attaching the joined strips to the quilt top (being careful not to stretch them), cut the excess length even with the adjacent sides of the quilt top.*

6. Attach the two side joined border strips to the blocks. Remember that the dark strips are next to the blocks.

7. Your quilt top is ready to be hand quilted, machine quilted or tied.

8. Finish the edges with a ¼″ binding.

COURTHOUSE STEPS

Maker unknown, c.1880-1900. Collection of Robert and Ardis James.

12″ Block	CRIB	WALL	TWIN	DOUBLE/QUEEN	KING
Finished size	39″ × 56″	56″ × 56″	73″ × 90″	90″ × 90″	90″ × 107″
Blocks set	2 × 3	3 × 3	4 × 5	5 × 5	5 × 6
Total blocks	12	18	40	50	60
Number of blocks to cut for half blocks	3	4	7	8	9

Note: Border fabric is figured on lengthwise cuts.

Center square	1/8	1/4	1/4	3/8	3/8
Logs: light and dark, *each*	1 1/8	2	3 3/8	4 1/4	5 1/8
Inside border	1 3/4	1 3/4	2 5/8	2 5/8	3
Middle border	1 3/4	1 3/4	2 5/8	2 5/8	3
Outside border	1 3/4	1 3/4	2 5/8	2 5/8	3
Backing	1 3/4	3 1/2	5 1/2	8	9 1/2
Binding	3/8	1/2	5/8	5/8	3/4

CUTTING YOUR FABRIC

Use Templates C1–C7

Center: Template C1, number of 2 1/2" squares	12	22	40	50	60
Template C2, light, number of 1 1/2" × 2 1/2" pieces	24	44	80	100	120
Template C3, light and dark, number of 1 1/2" × 4 1/2" pieces, *each*	24	44	80	100	120
Template C4, light and dark, number of 1 1/2" × 6 1/2" pieces, *each*	24	44	80	100	120
Template C5, light and dark, number of 1 1/2" × 8 1/2" pieces, *each*	24	44	80	100	120
Template C6, light and dark, number of 1 1/2" × 10 1/2" pieces, *each*	24	44	80	100	120
Template C7, dark, number of 1 1/2" × 12 1/2" pieces	24	44	80	100	120
Inside border:	Cut four 1 1/2"-wide lengthwise strips for all sizes.				
Middle border:	Cut four 1 1/2"-wide lengthwise strips for all sizes.				
Outside border:	Cut four 1 3/4"-wide lengthwise strips for all sizes.				
Backing: number of lengths	1	2	2	3	3

PUTTING IT ALL TOGETHER

1. Arrange your fabric pieces as shown on page 7.

2. Construct the required number of blocks (total blocks), using the *Courthouse Steps* Block technique.

3. For half blocks, carefully cut the required number of whole blocks in half diagonally, as shown.

4. For corner blocks, cut one whole block into quarters diagonally, as shown.

5. Join all whole blocks, half blocks and corner blocks together, in a diagonal setting, as shown. Double check the placement of the light and dark strips with the illustration before sewing.

6. Sew the three border strips for each side together lengthwise.

7. Attach the joined borders to each side of the quilt top.

8. Miter the corners and trim the excess border length.

9. Your quilt top is ready to be hand quilted, machine quilted or tied.

10. Finish the edges with a 1/4" binding.

This quilt's maker created the half blocks by cutting whole blocks in half diagonally and corner blocks by cutting whole blocks into quarters diagonally. Although this is not the accepted method of making these blocks, because it does not allow for seam allowance, this slightly smaller block is easier to construct and the small, hardly noticeable difference does not detract from the beauty of the quilt.

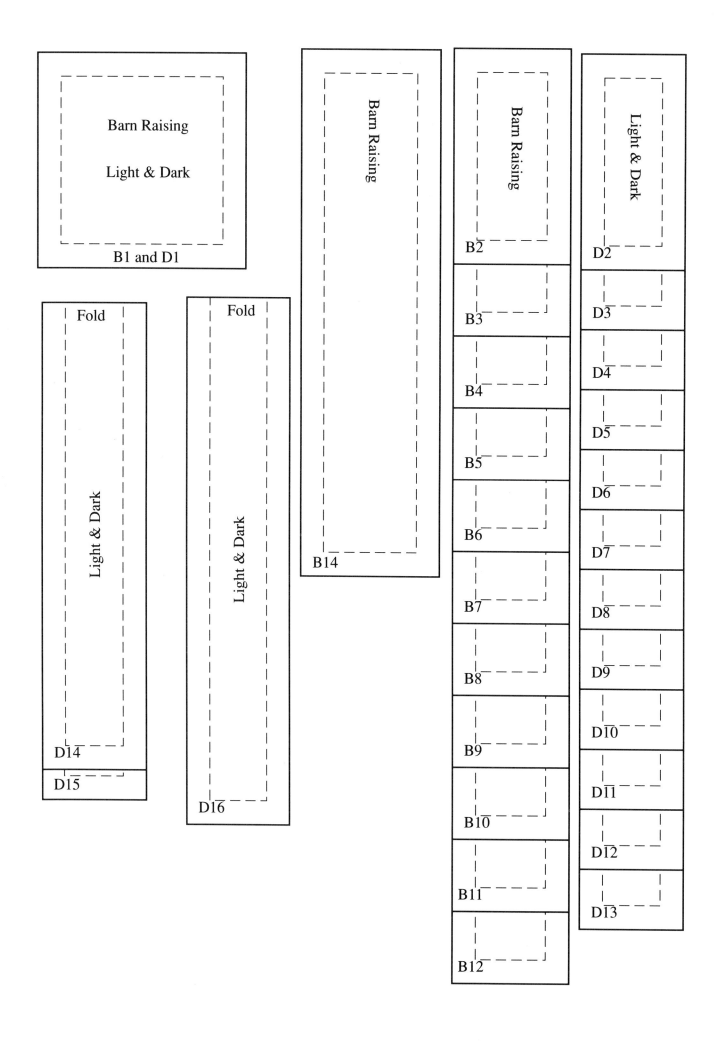

Barn Raising

Light & Dark

B1 and D1

Fold

Fold

Barn Raising

Barn Raising

Light & Dark

Light & Dark

Light & Dark

B14

B2

B3

B4

B5

B6

B7

B8

B9

B10

B11

B12

D2

D3

D4

D5

D6

D7

D8

D9

D10

D11

D12

D13

D14

D15

D16

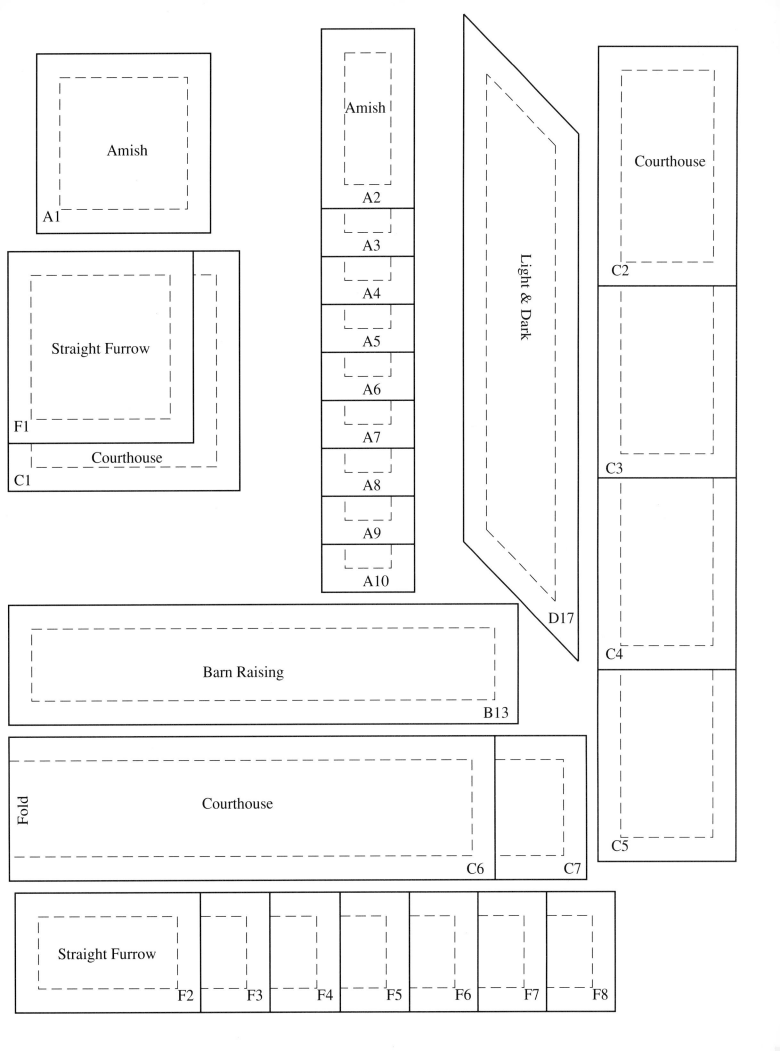

Amish

A1

Straight Furrow

F1

Courthouse

C1

Amish

A2

A3

A4

A5

A6

A7

A8

A9

A10

Light & Dark

D17

Courthouse

C2

C3

C4

C5

Barn Raising

B13

Fold

Courthouse

C6

C7

Straight Furrow

F2

F3

F4

F5

F6

F7

F8

Simply the Best

*W*hen we started our publishing efforts in 1983, we made one pledge to ourselves: to produce the finest quilt books imaginable. The critics and our loyal readers clearly believe that we're living up to that promise.

In a time when thin, 64-page quilt books with only staples to hold their pages intact and small numbers of color photos sell for as much as $19.95, we are proud that our books set a noticeably higher standard.

Books from The Quilt Digest Press are hefty, with many more pages and masses of color photos. They are printed on high-quality satin-finish paper and are bound with durable glues and spines to last a lifetime. The world's finest quilt photographer does all our work. A great design team lavishes its attention on every detail of every page. And the world's finest commercial printer sees to it that every book is a gem. Add knowledgeable authors with vital ideas and you, too, will say, "The Quilt Digest Press? Oh, they're Simply the Best."

Try another of our books. They're as good as the one in your hands. And write for our free color catalogue.

THE QUILT DIGEST PRESS

Dept. D
955 Fourteenth Street
San Francisco 94114